A TRIP AROUND THE WORLD
WONDERS AND PLACES ON EARTH

COLORING BOOK FOR KIDS AND ADULTS

GS COLORING

DESIGN

We love that you chose our book! Reading your reviews helps us to improve, if you can write yours we will really appreciate it!

INDEX

Printed in Great Britain
by Amazon

29707166R00051